/kenT youngstrom

**be something.
if you
want
to make
something.**

you want to be an artist? the untortured kind? then you might want to sit + read + listen to kenT youngstrom's startling advice about what it takes to be . . . an artist. and then get off your duff and do it! i chatted with kenT when he was starting out and selling just a couple of paintings a year. now, a few years later, he's shipping them out by the truckload. but it's not just about the sale. it's about the lifestyle. the freedom. the excitement. and how to make it all work for you - right now.

susan harrow, CEO of prsecrets.com, media coach, author of sell yourself without selling your soul

the single most creative person i know. he just happens to not be crazy. imagine that. read this book.

jennifer snyder, author of don't change the channel

be something. if you want to make something not only kickstarted my creative engine, but it set me on a new trajectory to lead my team by being the designer, leader, and person that I was created to be. listen to kenT - he knows – and lives – what he's talking about.

ryan hollingsworth, design + communications, elevation church, charlotte, nc

photograpy by allison fowler photograpy + christine szeredy photography

published in usa by kryout books

ISBN-13: 978-0692643860

printed in the united states of america

where the good stuff be /

thankful	7
introduction	8
notes	10
i don't know what to be	12
be surprising	19
be awake	23
be inspiring	25
be you	29
be non-traditional	34
be moving	37
be easy	39
be presentable	43
be a dishwasher	44
be repetitive	45
be generous	50
be unsuccessful	53
be honest	57
be blue	60
be obsessed	63
be now	66
be a star	70
be	72

thankful/

nicole. for letting me **be** even when i had no idea what that meant.

riley + jackson. for letting me know i'm not as cool as i think i am.

mom. for passing down your mad skills.

dad. for letting me take crayola one and two in college even though i'm sure you were wondering what i was going to do with it.

introduction /

by melissa cassera, *pr expert, business strategist, and screenwriter*

as a marketing consultant, i spend a lot of time teaching people how to **be**. be original. be helpful. be authentic. be obsession-worthy. be so good they can't ignore you.

when I met kenT it was like getting struck by lightening.

this guy just knows how to **be**.

my first experience with him was in a free class i was teaching to 1,100 entrepreneurs. you can imagine among 1,100 people it would be really ridiculously hard to stand out. especially online, in the middle of a facebook group that was moving so fast i could hardly keep my little fingers typing. as i was scrolling and connecting with my students, i noticed that every post had likes and comments, but one post had more likes and comments than anyone, and the number kept climbing.

here's what it said: i'm kenT, and i'm an artist. but not the tortured kind. i create one-of-a-kind images - no two are exactly the same. some are big. some are small. some have words. some have none. but what I really do is make people feel happy + free. they don't even have to know why. after all, happy + free is a great place to be.

people loved kenT's unusual "introduction" and took notice. i took notice. it **surprised** me. because it's rare to find a business owner who says his true purpose is to make people feel "happy and free." and you could feel his energy pour through his words, and you could see it in the photos of his paintings that he shared.

as the days went on, kenT's assignments stood out. always. he was so damn good that, throughout the class, other students were forfeiting their chance to win that day's prize and pleading with me to just "give it to kenT." and it wasn't just his talent that stood out. he took the time to cheer on his classmates. to share helpful and thoughtful comments. he lived and breathed his introduction. everyone knew it. there are so many ways to **be** it can be maddening. everywhere you turn there's someone telling you to "be" this or "be" that.

after getting to know kenT, striving to "be" just an ounce like him guarantees awesomeness. since he's too humble to include a "be kenT" chapter, this intro is my way of doing it for him.

xo,
melissa

notes /

a few quick notes.

presently i am on an endorphin high and believe that i have conquered the art world and that i will soon be a national treasure. or, on the flip side, i have spent too much time online, comparing my work and accomplishments to other artists i am jealous of. i am just like everyone else in that i struggle to find a balance. nameste on being in-between those two.

i only use lower case letters. get over it.

please don't drink soda. this is my one public service announcement.

i'm crawl in a ball + hide under the desk afraid every time i show something new. i am my work. it's called exposure for a reason. this fear includes letting anyone read these few words i have scribbled.

i don't know what to be /

i'm kenT, and i'm an artist. but not the tortured kind.

i think i've always been an artist. at least since people in social settings started introducing themselves and asking me what i do. but i was way too scared to say it so simply. i struggled to tell people who i was and what i did. i felt so compelled to validate myself that i crammed everything i had ever done or wanted to do into my basic description. i would probe into what i thought someone might need me to be before giving a full answer.

it often went something like, "i'm a graphic artist with a background in interior design, exhibit fabrication, painting, set design, marketing, and branding." a long-winded, confusing, and skeptical description of a design superhero. a sort of captain brand o' maker.

i had friends who would chuckle each time they heard me change my job description based on who i was talking to + what i thought i could get them to hire me for. i was so undecided in my own journey that i made it confusing for others to see what my particular set of skills actually were.

like a young boy raised by wolves, i believe much of this was forged by my surroundings. i had moved to a location where i was struggling to find full-time employment, was just starting out on my own, and was trying to make a name for myself in the community. i figured if i was everything to everyone, i would be much more in demand.

my family and i stayed afloat. it was a roller coaster ride of jobs and money coming in and propelling us to the top of the tracks, only to plummet, hands clenched on the bar, when there were no payments flowing in.

i took a night job and answered phones until odd hours in the evening while i worked on starting a design business during the day. i took not-so-glamorous jobs, such as marketing potatoes and made corporate flyers for convention-goers. i hustled + sold myself out to just about any job i could get. it is the part of the story no one wants to read. it's the part where you are not sure if it will all work. where you wonder if you are good enough. if you have what it takes. it is the part where the negative part of your thinking-path often winds and curves around the positive thoughts that keep you going. the thoughts that help put one foot in front of the other in hopes of a big break.

hard work and persistence would occasionally get us riding back up the big hill, and every so often the tracks even seemed smooth.

more than once i experimented with peeking into the corporate world and scanned job boards for full-time creative positions.

eventually, i made a big move from the midwest and headed south to take on a position of creative director for a new design firm. funny thing was, much like i was in my previous career, this firm was a bit undecided as to what it would be as well.

to make a crappy story seem a little less bathroom-like, i'll just say that within a year i was back on my own trying to find work as a graphic artist with a background in interior design, exhibit fabrication, painting, set design, marketing, and branding. i even added house painter, wallpaper hanger, soccer coach, and general do-anything-errand-boy to that list.

cue soft depressing music, perhaps with the gruntal twang of gavin degraw.

i had been painting for quite some time and had sold a few pieces to friends and family members, as well as participated in a couple of local shows. to be honest, most of my work was hanging in my own home or stashed away in the garage i occasionally used as a place to paint. i would fulfill a commission now and then, but honestly never answered the dreaded "what do you do?" question with "i'm an artist." even my neighborhood friends struggled to understand what kenT did for a living.

my neighbor, two doors down, had a summer get together one beautiful carolina summer evening. the kind with lemonade for the kids and lemonade with the good stuff for the adults, along with grilled meats, corn on the cob, and a vicious game of kick ball in the back yard. one of the party goers was the neighbor's best friend since high school and a self-proclaimed artist agent. i met her showcasing a notebook of images from one of her artists (who is now a great friend as i could fill a book with stories of both success and failure, as well as busts that, through no fault of my own, turned into accidental successes. it would include winning a blue ribbon for best booth, but not selling one item at the first art show i ever attended, or forgetting i was the live entertainment at a wedding and nearly missing the event entirely. in fact, i did fill a small book with such stories. *be something if you want to make something* is really a guide as to how i went from selling at one small school show to national sales, licensing deals, works in national publications, and more. i continue to learn every single day.

your dream is delightfully do-able. this is one of my favorite quotes on a set of art prints i collaborated on with the supremely talented writer, alexandra franzen. do-able. perhaps not a proper word, but it captures the most important part of your dream.

it's the do-ing.

dreams are easy. i have lots of them.

unfortunately i didn't put in the time to learnt to hit the curve ball, no one wants to hear me sing or see me dance, and i've been told i'm too nice to be on reality tv. i could work on those things over and over again, but churning that type of cream repeatedly would never produce any butter. to be honest, all the quotes on hard work and hustling look great on your wall or in your social media feed, but they will not make you a pop star either. i know a lot of hard working people that struggle mightily. you may be one of them. at times, i am too.

as i stood and chatted with folks at those first art shows about what i paint, why i paint, and how i paint, i realized something. if i wanted to be an artist, i needed to be an artist. it was about be-ing. not just do-ing.

is there a difference?

i think so. i can "do things" all day long. i can make lists. i can do invoicing. i can do packing and shipping. i can do the laundry. that, however, does not make me an organizer, an accountant, a shipper, or a dry cleaner.

if you want to be an artist, a maker, a creator, or a fill-in-the-blank, you have to be one with everything you have. it is not a job. it is who and what you are. it is your obsession. if you want people to be so obsessed with what you do that they are willing to pay anything for it, you sure as heck had better be over the edge, strung out on exhilaration, and obsessed with what you do.

so you want to be an artist? me too. i'm kenT, and i'm an artist.

the following are few verbs of being that will set you on your way. some of these i am naturally gifted at. most of them i am not.

it's time to be. /

**wake up.
get off the couch.
work your backside off.
show up on time.
surprise somebody.**

me.

be surprising /

it's 7:30 pm, and i'm on the couch, flipping through instagram photos like my thumb has been injected with oxycontin. i glance through design magazines, and, while visually impressive, they all seem to land in the recycling bin.i'm assuming the bachelorette is kissing another dude and handing out more roses, someone is looking for a new house, or someone is naked and afraid. or maybe someone is kissing someone looking for a new house but is naked and afraid. i'm not sure. i can't keep it all straight. the flat screen remains off.

so what am i looking for?

i'm desperately seeking for something to grab my attention. it doesn't even have to be susan.

what i want, what i really really want is for something to reach out, grab me, and pin me to the wall.

something to make my thumb halt. maybe even reverse. something more than just pretty. i need something to jump off the screen and into my repetitive thought system. i need a secret admirer. a mysterious fedex box. an exotic rendezvous.

or really all i need is a simple surprise.

something unexpected, a little out of the ordinary, something i don't experience everyday.

want to make stuff for a living?

wake up. get off the couch. work your backside off. show up on time. and most importantly… surprise somebody.

simple concept. simple idea. sometimes, simply hard to do.

surprising someone really is what this whole journey of be-ing someone who is noticed is all about.

as an artist i fight with the typical starving artist stereotype. i am expected to fit into a mold. it's a "scattered, out-of-the-box, running late, torn-jeans wearing, messed-up hair" kind of mold.

consider austin, texas. an incredible place to live + create. it is vibrant, artistic, and labeled as the live music capital of the world. take a journey there during the south by southwest music festival, and you will be overwhelmed. you may initially even be surprised. most likely by the size and sheer abundance of things to see and do.

but look closely. what is surprising? with that many artists and artistic people all in one area, none of them really seem to stand out from one another. everyone looks like an artist or a band member. it's like the time i descended the stairs in skinny jeans to the question from my son of "hey dad, you in the band?"

i think spike lee playing mars blackman in the first nike air jordan commercial got it wrong. it has nothing to do with the shoes.

if you want to make and make a living at this, you have to surprise people. not with how you look, but with your product, your personality, and your service. surprise does not mean crazy or overboard obnoxious - it means to exceed their expectations.

the corporate world has an absurd way of gauging their employees' performances.

at year end reviews, employees are given marks of either "does not meet," "meets," or "exceeds" expectations. based on those reviews, bonuses are given, promotions are made, etc. employees work all year just to get one of those credits on their records. those that "meet" expectations just keep riding the train. those that do not are given a second and sometimes third chance to bring up their marks. those that are marked "exceeds" (which are few and far between) are considered stars within the company and often get a new title (oooooh - aaahhh, yeah!) and perhaps a bigger bonus. for the most part, employees "meet" expectations, and things continue to move along as is.

as an entrepreneur or business owner / maker, we are not given such reviews. we are only offered two possible marks. either yes. or no. and we are given those reviews on a daily basis.

yes. yes, i will buy from you again, work with you again, forward you to a friend, and carry a torch for you.

or a no. h - e - double - hockey - sticks no, i won't buy from you again. in fact, i'll tell others not to as well. see that review - you suck. no stars for you. a rating of one. there is no second or third chance. if you do not deliver, you lose.

clients are not your corporate team managers - they will not keep you around because it is easier than finding someone new or it is risky to make changes. they will drop you. i'm sure of it because i do. i'm not good with second chances on customer service. i've walked out of a small shop when the owner was too chatty on the phone to help me. i took my business elsewhere. i refuse to purchase art supplies at a big box store minutes from my home, and instead drive farther, because it is so slow and has an aura of malaise. i'm certain you have stories of poor results in which you have taken your business somewhere else. you may not have the same i-won't-shop-there list as i do, but i'll bet you have one.

unless you exceed their expectations, which are high, customers / clients will move on to the next person on their lists.

do more for clients or potential clients than they expect. **be nice. be helpful.**

treat them as you would your best friend. it surprises people. /

dear left side of my brain:

please leave me alone. i'm tired of your nagging.

your constant tapping of the taboo game buzzer is getting old.

i am well aware that my current idea has a slim-to-none chance of working.

i realize that no one to my knowledge has done this before with any degree of success.

i am fully in the know that oil + water do not mix. nor do acrylic paint + oil paint. i'm smart enough to figure out the comparison there.

but would you for a second cease and desist?

if i had listened to you before, i would not have started this whole artist thing in the first place. i wouldn't make booklets of my work and send it to folks i have no business sending them to.

i would answer "no" when asked if i could "make three hundred of those."

i'd still be working out of my garage.

i'd never do anything for free.

i would have never figured out that cattle markers can be used as oil pastels. or that roofing paper makes a great surface for painting.

i would have never left the lids off my paint jars to harden the paint until it was almost unusable to create texture.

please leave me alone left side.

be awake /

get out of bed.

yep. get your groggy backside up and moving.

most of us like to sleep in - dread the getting out of bed routine. i was in the camp of more sleep, more sleep, more sleep for nearly all my life. i tried for years to get up earlier + work out in the morning, study, or just do anything early.

nothing worked.

until. . . i started leading a neighborhood exercise group. the only way i can get out of bed as early as i do is to have others counting on me.

so find a partner. have them call you - or meet them - or start a neighborhood work out group - nothing bad can come of that. coincidentally, i'm really telling you to get out of bed, because i can directly correlate my little business taking off with the time i started putting my feet on the floor earlier than i had before.

i now have two more hours to do what was otherwise occupying my late morning. i sleep better and more restful. i'm locked-in at the start of the work day. to be honest, i just feel better. i'm going to go hard-core on you. i tried the 15 min. increment thing - doesn't work. so just go for it. pick a time. mine is 5 am for a 5:45 work out. and do it - it will suck at first - but do it for a few weeks with your accountability peeps. you will soon have the frustrating problem of being angry at yourself when you do sleep in.

so yeah - wake up + get out of bed.

no one's tomb stone reads: " i should have slept more."

be awake. it surprises people. /

be inspiring /

people don't follow products or join revolutions if they don't have a cause.

what is your cause? what is your mission?

think of all the people you follow socially or make your head snap in the grocery line magazine rack. each and every one of those individuals has a story or a reason why they capture your attention.

you don't follow products or widgets, no matter how cool they are.

i get dmv-line-anxious when i think of people asking me the meaning behind my work or why i do what i do. does it really matter? all i want to do is paint.

but it does matter if i want to do this for a living, if i want to have a following - a following that pays for the product i make.

the last thing i want to do is stand in front of my work and talk about it. the right-brain side of me says if you can't figure out what i was thinking - or if you aren't sure if you like it by just looking at it - then it is not the right piece for you. i lack a desire to convince you to take home a piece unless you are totally obsessed with it.

then it hit me one day. like a ronda rousey right hook. the goal is not to make buyers fall in love with just one of my pieces. i need to make them obsessed with the whole package. the story. i need them to get behind me and support my mission.

so what is my mission? how did i figure it out? as an artist, i seem to be all over the place.

what am i truly passionate about? what makes me laugh, cry, get angry - sends me into a rant?

who do i look up to?

my good friend, melissa cassera, the one from the generously nice introduction, says it this way in her *obsessed* workshop. . .

your movement doesn't necessarily have to be "innovative" or "crazy-

original" or "flashy" or "provocative." more than anything else, it just has to be simple.

simple to say.

simple to understand.

simple for your audience to talk about, share and repeat.

don't make your movement more complicated than it needs to be.

simple is good.

in the words of the aforementioned alexandra franzen - brevity is sexy.

and speaking of sexy, can someone please take on these as a mission? i'd find it hotter than a scarlett johansson lip-bite.

mandatory use of turn signals or your car will implode.

stores remaining closed all of thanksgiving.

all processed foods being placed above the middle shelf, so they are harder to reach.

eliminating the words multi-million dollar contract from all sports news.

stun gun availability for all those standing in the walk portion of the moving walkway.

officially change the name of home and garden television channel to boring-butt real-estate channel featuring lazy americans actually watching other people look for a house.

start a movement. be inspiring. it surprises people. /

**i'm on a mission
to make the walls
of your home, office,
or secret lair
as amazing as
you are.**

me

dear folks who assume i pull creativity from my backside at will:

i am not a polaroid camera. i am not instant.

in fact, i am not any more creative than you are.

i am fearless (or at least i want you to think that).

i started out with the same insane amount of creativity as you did.

don't believe me?

volunteer at my kids' art camp. see what is inside those crazy, unaltered, uninhibited little brains. see their eyes light up when i tell them the first rule of art camp is "that there are no rules."

be you /

logos are awesome.

if you are a giant company that resembles a red fruit that grown on trees, if you sell burgers, or if you are a 14-year-old girl and need validation. i remember my jr. high days. for reasons from acne breakouts and other weird body changes to emotional instability, i would choose to skip those torture hours completely.

one thing i have a strong memory of is having to have the right logos on my clothes. i just wasn't cool if there wasn't a horse with a polo player, an s on my watch with its proper rubber band protector, a bugle boy patch, an OP, a nike symbol, and so on. yes, you can now figure my age.

to this day, i have developed a hatred for horses, alligators, whales, and swooshes.

we, the billboard-touting junior highers, of course graduate to adulthood and continue to validate ourselves with our favorite branding marks. we so often replace individual style with a khaki collision of branded wear that proves that we can follow in line and obtain what the guy next to us can - or can not.

as my mother would say - "for pete's sake" - be your own logo.

what do you stand for?

who are you behind that shirt?

would or should i wear something you are wearing - not literally, but figuratively?

what is your mark?

if someone were to sum you up in an image, what would it be?

try this. pretend you are walking into a prestigious ad agency to meet with their hot, young design team. they want to brand you - funds are not an issue. this is pro bono work.

how do you start the meeting?

what do you tell them about yourself to have them capture you and everything you stand for?

think big picture. no one cares if your favorite color is pink, that you adore tulips, love long walks on the beach, and that you think prince is the greatest rock star of all time. (well, maybe the prince thing.)

think more like i'm purple rain in a world of storm clouds. i look for the good in others and rejoice more in their successes than my own.

they won't have a long time to meet with you. they have a lot of clients on the books - you will need to be precise and succinct. go. come up with it. then be it - but never let anyone else wear it.

be you. sing like pretty woman in the bathtub. it surprises people. /

dear left side of the brain:

it's me again. seriously, please go away.

but just for a bit. i'm going to need you tomorrow to send some email responses.

to make a list of pieces going to the next sale.

to help with shipping, invoicing and a bit of the marketing.

perhaps your left-sidedness could make a weekly visit to do the said boring tasks i hate doing.

that would be nice.

just note, i'll probably change the schedule on you.

**every
artist
is
first
an amatuer.**

ralph waldo emerson

be non-traditional /

traditions are great. every other thanksgiving my crazy family gathers, and we have our own olympic games. everyone brings or creates his or her own quick game for the competition. we spend two days competing, laughing, challenging judgments, and overall having an "i-don't-want-this- to-end" good time. we compete in everything from rolling quarters into fork tongs to tossing playing cards into watermelon halves. it's a tradition we all look forward to.

however, traditions can also be inhibiting or downright unnecessary and often become patterns we aren't quite sure why exist. for example…

can anyone please tell me why major league baseball managers still wear uniforms?

do we really need to see these men, well past their prime, wearing what looks like a clown suit on them as they stroll to the pitcher's mound at a leisurely pace (about the only pace there is to baseball)?

if rules were made to be broken, then so are traditions.

traditions can give you comfort and let you feel a sense of place. just be careful not to let them dictate that you follow the path you are used to "just because. . . tradition." you are not a bearded fiddler dude singing and jumping from rooftops wearing lederhosen.

could family olympics be improved? can you have breakfast for dinner? does the manager have to wear a uniform? yes, absolutely, and absolutely not!

don't step in line just because it is the way it has always been done. don't be afraid to change your old habits and start new ones. walk away from the wrist bands – take off the spikes and step into a new part of the journey. you can't be a player forever – sometimes the uniform does not make the man.

anyway… we can save the baseball rant for another day. what are the traditions or patterns that are holding you back? are you the artist who says he or she can only work at night? are you stuck using the same colors over and over? when you pick up a brush, does a face always come out? do you use words to cover up the fact that you don't know what else to do?

try working at different hours of the day until you find your peak time – and every so often mix it up. i love a routine and find it comforting to know what i will be doing next – but sometimes my rut can turn into... a rut.

are you in a routine or tradition of purchasing the same materials to use for every project or commission?

i found there is more to work on than water color paper – or canvas. more to paint with than art store tubes. more to color with than oil pastels.

i broke my habit and visit the local home improvement store to mix things up. i found new materials to work with. go outside you can go outside of your industry and it's world to find new things.

you + your habits + your routine all need to be hacked. your journey needs another path. even if it's going smoothly. challenge yourself to do something different every once in a while.

so often we say it's about the journey.

maybe the journey isn't always about making something.

perhaps it's all about unmaking everything that isn't really you, so you can become what you were suppose to be in the first place.

be nontraditional. start a new path. it surprises people. /

dear midnight hour:

you suck. i should be asleep. i should not be getting my second wind.

you are like red bull without the crash. well, actually you do have a crash. a hard one.

why do you turn me on. is it the crisp breeze you bring to the studio with the dock door open? is it the fact that i'm energized like i'm weirdly thrown into an empty swimming pool and made to riff with a secretly cool acapella group? oh wait, that's the movie my daughter is watching.

or is it just the fact that if i'm up at this werewolf hour, i'm probably behind on a project and forcing myself to stay up and work my way through something?

either way, let's continue our love/hate relationship.

be moving /

i hate flying. if the timeframe is even remotely close, i'll drive every time. i have no john madden fear of it. i just hate it. from the arriving early, to the security line with the dude behind me who has no clue about personal space, to the hoards of idiots that stand up and crowd the entrance when the attendant is only calling for those needing extra assistance, to the odor-challenged individual i usually seem to sit next to, and so on and so forth. i loathe it.

and... would someone please tell the very important person who has apparently carried on the world cure for cancer in his oversized roll-on that it is not going to fit in the overhead compartment - no matter what direction he tries to turn it.

seriously, we are all going to the same place. we will all get there. even the ones in row thirty-six who immediately stand to exit once the plane has landed. where do these folks think they are going? trust me - i'm in a hurry - we are all in a hurry. how about a little courtesy and personal space, please?

yep - flying sucks - and so do most of the people flying with you. sound like your everyday environment? people around you standing and blocking your exit? guy next to you need to take a shower? not enough elbow room to move around? people in a hurry to get somewhere they really aren't ready to be yet? baggage holding you back?

don't fly. . . drive. walk. run. rv. rideshare. take the long way. do it yourself. find a co-pilot. find a different way.

use these metaphors as you will. find a new way to get there. wherever there is.

move. move on.

be moving. it surprises people. /

dear ana + cooper dogs:

thanks for keeping all my secrets. thanks for not telling everyone most of the pieces start out as crap. or that i paint over almost everything.

thank you for keeping to yourself that i sit around way more than i want you to think i do. that i snack all day long. that i'm not as cool as the photos show i am. that my hair is usually a mess. that i rarely shave. that i wear the same jeans for extended periods of time.

thank you for keeping a watchful eye on me. for snuggling close when i'm typing. for barking when i get a visitor. for keeping kids at art camp entertained.

thank you for keeping all my secrets, even if you require treats.

be easy /

would you like a carwash?

have a rewards card? zip code? want a coupon? mother's maiden name? first street your second cousin's high school mascot lived on?

seriously, i'm just trying to get gas here.

why is it so difficult to get service sometimes?

i'm standing, card in hand ready to pay - ready to buy - ready to spend my hard-earned money. take it. take it, and let me get on with my day.

seems like an easy concept.

as merchants we make it so cumbersome sometimes.

here is some simple advice. given with a simple question.

would you buy from you?

take a credit card - even if it cost you a small percentage of the sale. put the price of shipping into the product, so shipping is not extra. if it breaks, replace it. if it's wrong, fix it.

be easy to work with. be easy to refer. i don't give this advice to my daughter, but i do to you. be easy.

have you ever seen the scottish keg toss competition where the guys in skirts, i mean kilts, toss kegs over increasingly high walls? i am convinced shipping companies play similar games with my packaged paintings. i've given up on insuring them because it is denied every time. apparently unless ansel adams takes photos of the packaging, all claims will be denied. that's not the point of this story however. i have on separate occasions had paintings both stabbed and snapped in half.

on both of those occasions, i gained clients for life by simply fixing the problem at no cost or no hassle to the client. no hemming and hawing about let me check and file a claim and get back to you. no. on the phone i took care of it the first time.

client one got a youtube video and a repair kit, because she wanted to fix it herself. i did not know her at the time or know she would soon be a great client and business friend. since the dexter-like box-stabbing incident, i was the initial artist on her quote-sharing app (which was launched at harpo studios). she also has since purchased multiple pieces and promoted my work to countless business connections.

client two got his package picked up the next day and returned to him in about a week or so - fixed and ready to hang. he also got a small painting just for the delay and the hassle.

was all this convenient for me? absolutely not. pain in the derrière. but the end result sure was a win - win.

take care of your customer as if they were your mom. (minus the discount and, well, frankly the hassle that would be.) they will tell other customers as if they were your mom too. you know - like every time she talks to them!

be easy. be nice to your mom. it surprises people. /

dear instagram.

go away. along with the insecurities you bring.

but help me sell stuff, please.

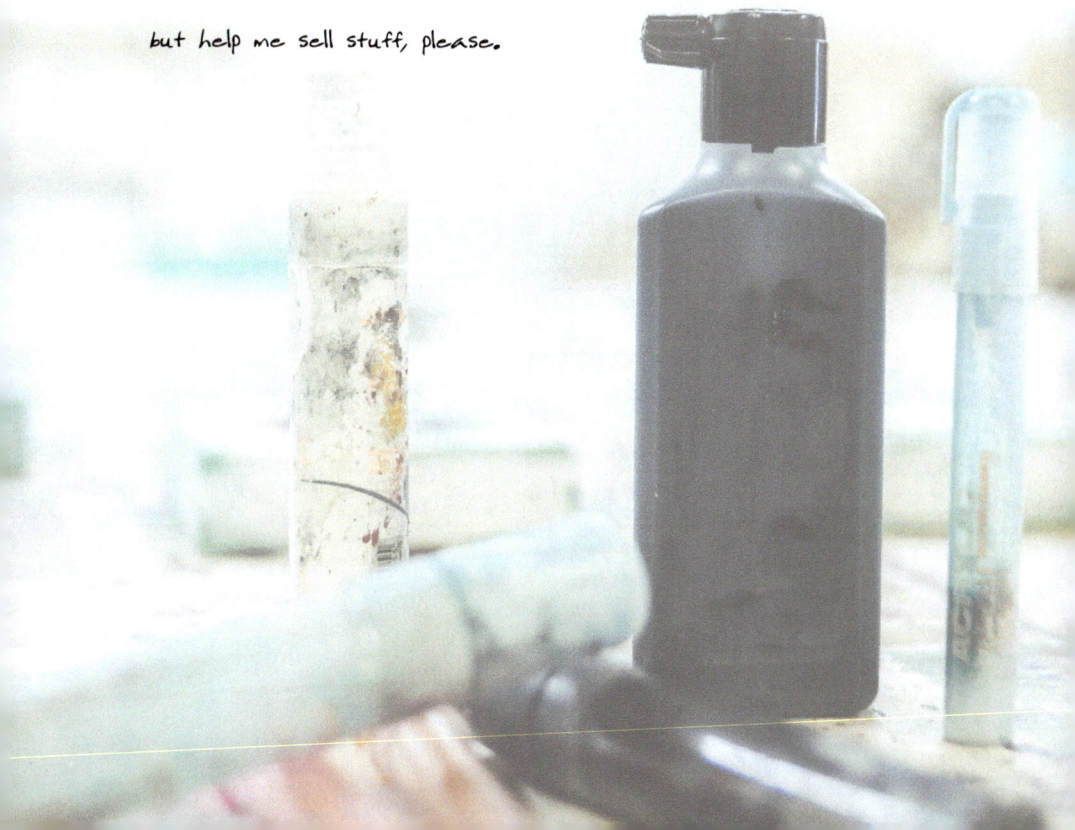

unmake
everything that isn't
really you,
so you can become
what you were
supposed to be
in the first place.

me again

be presentable /

flip-flops are awesome. if you're in cancun. or trying to avoid a foot fungus while taking a shower at the gym. anywhere else - no.

yes. i said it. if you are a dude - flip-flops are out. i can not think of a reason i ever want to see your hairy, messed-up feet. especially in a meeting - be it office or morning coffee - or a studio visit.

some may disagree - and i'm fine with that.

my point really is not so much about the shoes of death, but about being professional. i am a maker - meaning i make things and present them to others in various ways.

it can be cool to be an artist and show up in jeans and casual wear at times. but know the limits - it is your business. find the balance of being yourself and being presentable. if you are unsure, lean heavily towards the presentable. flip-flops are not presentable.

the flip-flop rant is over, but apply it as you will.

ripped jeans - great in studio + photo shoots. use your judgment elsewhere.

backwards cap - seriously? polo shirt festooned with alligator - see "be you" chapter.

yoga pants - invented by God to accentuate his creations, but perhaps could be traded for something else when presenting work.

i am all for individuality - i usually have blue hair or some sort of detail going on with my look. but keep in mind your target market. who are you selling to? who is buying your work? what makes them comfortable?

be presentable. wear shoes. it surprises people. /

be a dishwasher /

go ahead. pre-rinse that plate.

really. what is this, 1984? are you telling me i can kick a soccer ball that tells me its own speed, trajectory, and spin; unlock my house with my phone; and my car will park itself, but i can't put my plate of spaghetti into the dishwasher without rinsing it first? am i correct in that it is called a dishwasher? or is it just misnamed and should be referred to as a dishwetter? not to be confused with bed wetter (a different book altogether in the self-help section).

all this to say... be what you say you are. if you are going to be a dishwasher - wash the freak'n dishes. if you are going to be a writer - write. if you are going to be a business coach - coach. if you are going to be a maker - make! make lots. then make more.

seriously. what is the first step for making + selling?

making! so make stuff. make lots of stuff. make more than you think you need to make.

you will be ignored. you will be told no. you will fail. your work will not be chosen. others will sell more. you will need money. you will be exhausted.

you will trip. you will fall. you will break. you will feel small. you will want to quit. you will want help.

you will never want to do anything else.

don't give up.

be the classic comeback to all put downs.

i'm rubber and you're glue. whatever you say bounces off me and sticks to you. it is not all peonies and pixie dust.

you will have to bounce back. more than once.

when you do, bounce back hard. fearless. fierce. without inertia.

to quote the best line in any of the batman movies:

"why do we fall bruce?"

"so we can learn to pick ourselves up."

my favorite stories are the one's where i hear about those who "have made it" after almost giving up.

be one of my favorite stories.

be who you say you are. be a dishwasher. it surprises people. /

be repetitive/

develop a routine. do it again.

i ate peanut butter + jelly sandwiches for lunch every day of my entire school career. i think maybe a finger-count of times i took leftover pizza. is this a little strange? yes. do i still eat pb & j? yes, however, now it is whole wheat bread, almond butter, and fruit spread. to me, a routine can be essential to your success.

currently my alarm chimes some upbeat tune at 5:00 am. i am starting some sort of crazy body-movement exercise by 5:45 or 6:00, depending on the day. afterwards I generally eat one of three things for breakfast. i'm out the door with the kids by 8:15 unless it's tuesday, which is bagel day and we leave 20 minutes earlier. after the ride, which is my favorite part of the day, i drop them off and head to the studio and am generally there from 9:00 until 4:00. five days a week. my nighttime ritual doesn't change much either.

as an artist, i think it is assumed that i am chaotic, unplanned, and live on a diet of unpredictability and a wild, orgasmic release of energy whenever i need to create.

that sounds movie-script romantic, but it is indeed no way to conduct a body of work that makes for a successful venture.

my pleasure is the pattern. it's doing it again. then again.

i'm a fighter. i'm driven. i hit the bag and get in the ring over and over.

not literally - but every day i'm there.

the pleasure of the pattern is the result.

the pattern may change, but it's all part of me. it's not a mix of plaid and stripes, but rather a mix of subtle textures and colors.

we have discussed my morning pattern previously. eventually i end up in my studio with the dogs, ana + cooper.

in that big box of paint. i have the freedom to insert new things each day as part of the pattern. i can even reward myself with breaks just for pleasure.

maybe a nap or a quick workout. i can paint something that has not been ordered, walk the dogs, text friends, take photos, crank spotify, juggle the soccer ball, downward dog my way to a little inspiration, or just jump around. jump around. jump up. jump up. and get down.

be repetitive. be boring even. it surprises people. /

dear facebook.

pound sand.

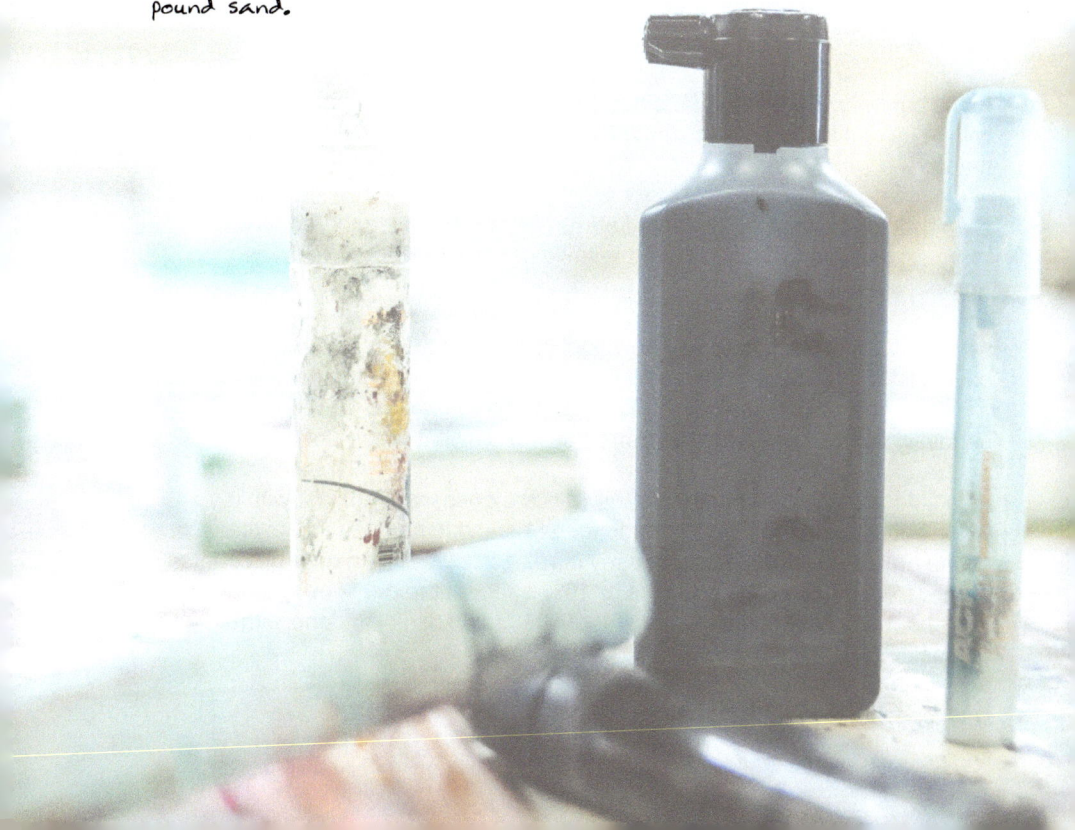

be generous/

give it away. give it away. give it away now.

i think i'm a generous person. until i meet someone who is really generous - or who gives me something unexpected.

i used to always think that when i became richy, rich, rich i would give things away. then it hit me one day. what am i waiting for? when will i ever reach that stage, and why will my mindset all of a sudden change? so i decided i wasn't waiting anymore.

i sent off a simple instagram request asking folks to send me a name of someone who needed a little sunshine in his or her day. i said i would choose a name and send them some real art. the flood gates didn't open, but i did receive several names and brief stories on why their friend could use a pick-me-up. i had trouble deciding who to choose - so i made something for all of them. i couldn't have had a better time making those pieces and sending them off.

to my surprise, i had those who nominated their friends blowing up my phone with texts and instant messages about the impact my simple gesture had made.

all of that led to another program i started in my local neighborhood where i give art away to those who need a smile or could never afford it. my cup runneth over.

i am telling you this just to say how cool i am. i don't want you to think i'm not saying it for that reason. kind of like using the hash tag #humbled.

seriously though. be giving. be generous. i promise it will return to you.

as a side note, i have a base of fans who are obsessed, not just with my work, but with the message and the ideas behind it. so i don't do giveaways online anymore. i'd rather service my current followers than offer discounts to new folks. i don't offer coupons or 10% off (am i the only one who ignores just about any sale unless it starts at 50%?), and i think i'm done with contests.

i'm just going to give things away.

it makes me feel good. it makes my work feel good.

be generous. be a giver. it surprises people. /

be unsuccessful/

the word success is stupid and supremly sucks silly putty.

success really isn't even in my vocabulary, and, in my opinion, should be removed from yours. success is similar to one of my least favorite words in the english language - "edgy." what is edgy? i can guarantee that at least ninety percent of those who have ever asked me for something edgy did not really want what i would consider edgy. they just wanted a little something above mamby-pamby milktoast normal. at the same time, my edgy is far below many artist's definition. it is truly a word that can only be understood by the speaker.

same for success. my definition is different than yours and can change based upon the situation. be it business, academics, or athletics, everyone has a different idea of what success is.

instead, let's strive for taking steps to ensure we get to experience the world in the way we want to.

many of us define the word "success" with numbers. those numbers can be dollars and cents or quantities sold. or maybe numbers of things we acquire.

i prefer to think of it in terms of my experiences. am i doing the things i want to do with those i want to do them with? if i am, then i can count that as what i want to be doing.

it is not a comparison of what i have or what others are doing in their posts + tweets. it is an experience. a memory. a moment here and now that i can fully embrace without having to take a picture. (put the camera phone down people.) it's in my mind - never to be taken away by someone else.

work for what no one can take away.

i'm pretty sure most of the stuff you acquire won't fit in your casket anyway.

be experience-based. be in the moment. it surprises people. /

**make them so
obsessed with
what you do,
that they are willing
to pay
anything for it.**
melissa cassera

be honest/

share your story - unashamed.

your past is just a story; it should render no power for your future.

to me my story is bland and unexciting. it goes something like this according to my website...

i started painting several years ago, in design school, without any big plans or ambitions. it was hard, unpredictable, time-consuming — and the best thing ever. by the end of day one, i was hooked.

one gallery show led to another, and before long i was selling paintings to friends, family, + a handful of local fans.

local sales turned into national sales. national sales turned into licensing deals. bulk orders from cb2 came knocking, along with flash sales at gilt.com, pops-ups in people magazine, and flattering attention from a couple of those "home makeover" reality tv shows.

one day, i woke up and realized: "huh … guess i'm a full-time artist now."

i grinned. and then put brush to canvas again.

the now story.

i live in north carolina with my (amazing) family.

i wake up at 5 am most mornings, work out, whirl the kids off to school, check my computer for new orders, plant myself in the center of (at least) ten half-covered canvases, and rarely stop moving 'til nightfall. i'm usually splattered in about seven colors of paint. it's a good way to move through the world.

life is complicated enough, so I keep my work simple.

i hope it makes you look. i hope it makes you smile.

i hope it makes you feel …
something you've been wanting to feel for a while.

to me the story is not james earl jones voice-over material or tedx worthy, but folks love to hear it.

they love to hear that i worked nights when i started out on my own. they want to know that i was perhaps in the same place they are or have debated between art supplies or food for the week.

my favorite stories revolve around celebrities or people i admire and their adventures to get where they are. what advice would they give? did they take it? ignore it?

was there a big break, a stroke of opportunity, or a combination of hard work, lost opportunities, and persistence? almost all are stories of the latter.

share your story. be human. be who you are. be honest. we don't need or want all the details - we don't have that long. hit the highlights and keep the drudgery to a minimum. let us know when and what you struggled with - let us know you figured it out and came out above the trash.

share your story. be honest. it surprises people. /

dear hollywood:

stop making me cry in front of my kids.

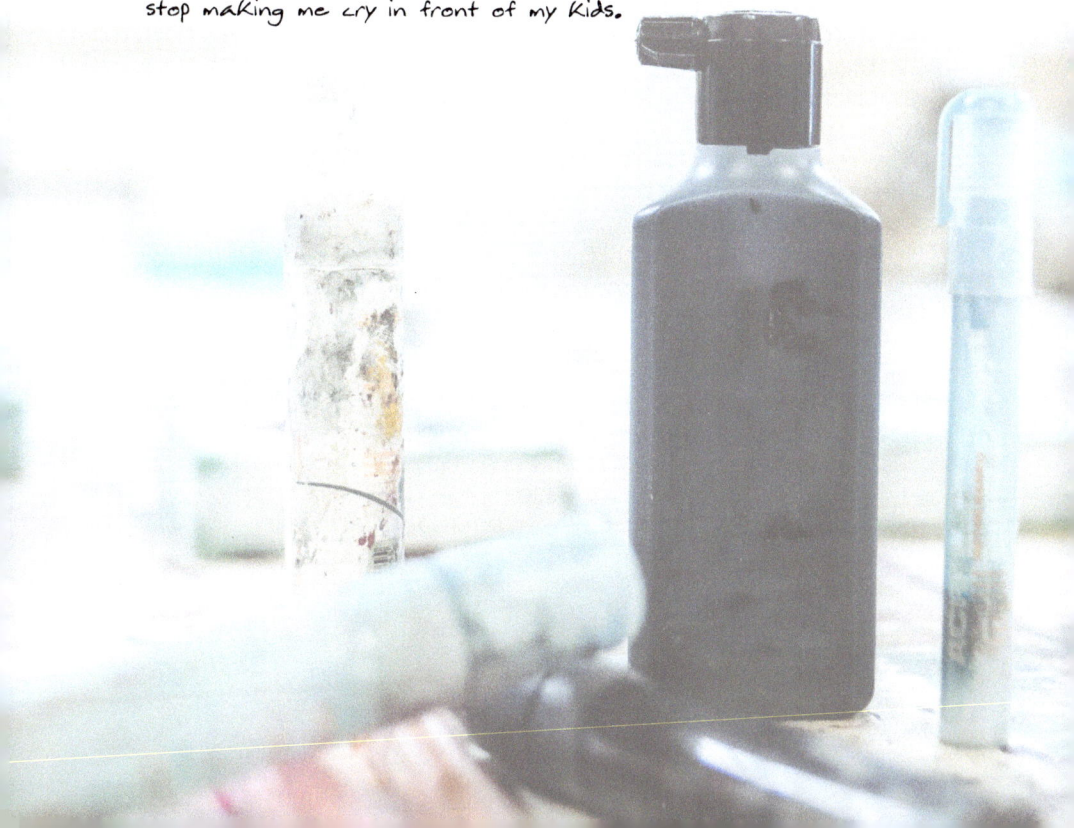

be blue/

have blue hair - or whatever it is that make you you.

i remember the drama kids from high school. or the art students from university. think of the stereotypes that stand out to you.

we all know folks who stand out for a variety of reasons. most of the time those folks are just out for attention. but do you have something that makes you you without defining you? do you have an individual style that your friends and acquaintances know is yours? this is different than something annoying or that makes others uncomfortable. i'm talking about something that makes you you and defines your style.

when we moved from the midwest to the south, i struggled a bit to fit in. my neighborhood wasn't exactly filled with artists. i didn't have the right job, drive the right car, or, for that matter, wear the same clothes.

i suppose i could have just gone to vineyard vines and purchased a new wardrobe, traded in the car, and corporatized myself. and, admittedly, to some extent i did.

it took what seemed like forever to be invited to the local poker game. i'll take some of the blame for this as i may not be the most social guy in the hood. it also took awhile for them to get who i was. why i had a small blue streak in my hair, was usually in jeans and a t-shirt, or covered in paint at the bus stop. i didn't force my style onto them or go all artsy and chastise them for what i saw as the status quo.

soon enough, they were asking me about my latest project, showing up at the art shows, asking to borrow my tools, and even inquiring about where to get some new clothes. i'll always remember my neighbor beaming at one of my shows when someone asked if he was one of my artist friends.

stay true without forcing it onto others. it surprises people. /

be obsessed/

binge.

netflix has turned television series watching into an art form. weekends, holidays, sick days, or just lazy days can easily become " i just binge watched season two of house of cards and now i feel like i actually voted for frank underwood."

while binging on a show may satisfy your dirty laundry gene, it is not going to do too much for your business bottom line. but that doesn't mean the phenomenon should be ignored. any artist will tell you there are high and low points of creative moments. those that capitalize on the highs and minimize the lows are the ones who are the masters.

binge on the highs. don't allow them to stop. keep pressing play (even when it asks, "are you still watching?"). do what you have to do to keep that momentum going. stay up all night if it's a short blast of energy. eat the same thing for a week if your paint is flying in the right direction. if your words just keep spilling out of you fingers onto the keyboard, then sit and order in. keep listening to whatever is in your headphones on repeat. take a break only when necessary. employ a can't stop, won't stop mentality.

i often get a painters high either mid-morning or late evening. i often start with grand plans to push through for a few more hours, jumping around and flinging paint and such. then the wall hits. "maybe i should take a break," i think. or check instagram. i need my sleep. normally i would agree and argue sleep is king. but it is those times that i push through that wall - keep painting, crank the music a little louder - that i find i grab a second wind, and the spattering, dripping, and twirling produce even greater effects.

i will always remember the night i found a new style by binging on a process. i was not especially on a high, but i had a large workload, an upcoming show, and i felt i needed something new. it was late. i was tired. but i kept going. perhaps there was an energy drink or a great song that got me going. for some reason, i grabbed the molding paste, which is like using a tub of heavy sour cream to thicken paint, and a big cow patty form accidentally dropped onto a painting. i mixed it a bit with the wet paint on the canvas and didn't really like how it looked. taking a few twirls around and looking for something to remove it with, i grabbed a comb i normally use for pulling + pushing epoxy resin around on canvas.

wham oh!

as i pulled the paste off the canvas with the comb, i fell in love with the texture it created and how it worked with the layers of paint underneath.

i've been using this technique ever since.

i would venture to say well over half of my work now contains this happy accident technique. i was binging on work. and frank underwood had nothing to do with it.

binge. keep pressing play. it surprises people. /

be a star/

taylor swift can't sing.

i can't draw.

ever heard this before? does it really matter?

absolutely not. no. it doesn't matter. she puts on a fantastic show + has taken care of her fans from day one before she was t-swizzle.

she puts out a positive message about being yourself to thousands of girls, no matter their age.

she sells out a concert in minutes, and, at this point, just about anything she touches turns to gold.

would she win a singing contest? no idea. does it really matter?

here's the point.

i'm a little jealous. if we are comparing myself to other artists, i would put myself in the "he can't sing" category. in a room filled with painters and art school graduates, i am in the back of the class test-scorewise.

test me with painting techniques, color mixing, blending and shading, perspective, form and function, etc., and i'll have to revert to peeking over the shoulder of the girl in front of me to pass the test.

however, i'll put on one heck of a show for you.

i'll give you rhythm and movement, and i can certainly compose color.

oh, and i'll compete with all of the rest of those goofy look'n painters until they are tired of seeing me. it will be like crossfit for artists. we can call it crosspaint or maybe paintfit. both of which sound as ridiculous as having to listen to a group of crossfitters discussing their wods, emoms, and various double-unders. so we will just paint and not call it anything.

if you want to do this making stuff thing for a living, it sometimes has little to do with the actual product.

making something and hanging it in a shop window, a gallery, or wherever you may find your work, does not a mortgage-paying career make.

taylor swift might not be able to sing, (not my line of thought) but i think she knows pretty well how to endorse a check.

i may not be the best "artist" you know, but i'm making a living out of it.

put on a show. be a star. it surprises people. /

dear exhaustion:

there are days i don't want to paint. have no desire to paint. would rather sit, sleep, surf, and waste away. anything except paint.

guess what i have to do. . . paint.

so i'll start slow. warm up. stretch. paint something other than what's due. my mind and body will take over and do it.

if i'm still not feeling it, i'll try just black and white.

or switch hands. paint fast.

turn the canvas sideways or upside down. start over.

red bull. change the music. no music. go outside. go for a walk. run. take a shower. use a color i never use. give myself a time limit.

yoga. paint and talk to a friend on speaker.

copy someone's work, then add my own touch. pretend the painting is a gift. scream at the work.

i'll paint more than one at a time. work on as many pieces at once as i can. one is too confining and too much pressure. i always paint two when commissioned to paint one.

i can paint over the one i don't like, or let the customer choose (they may buy both!).

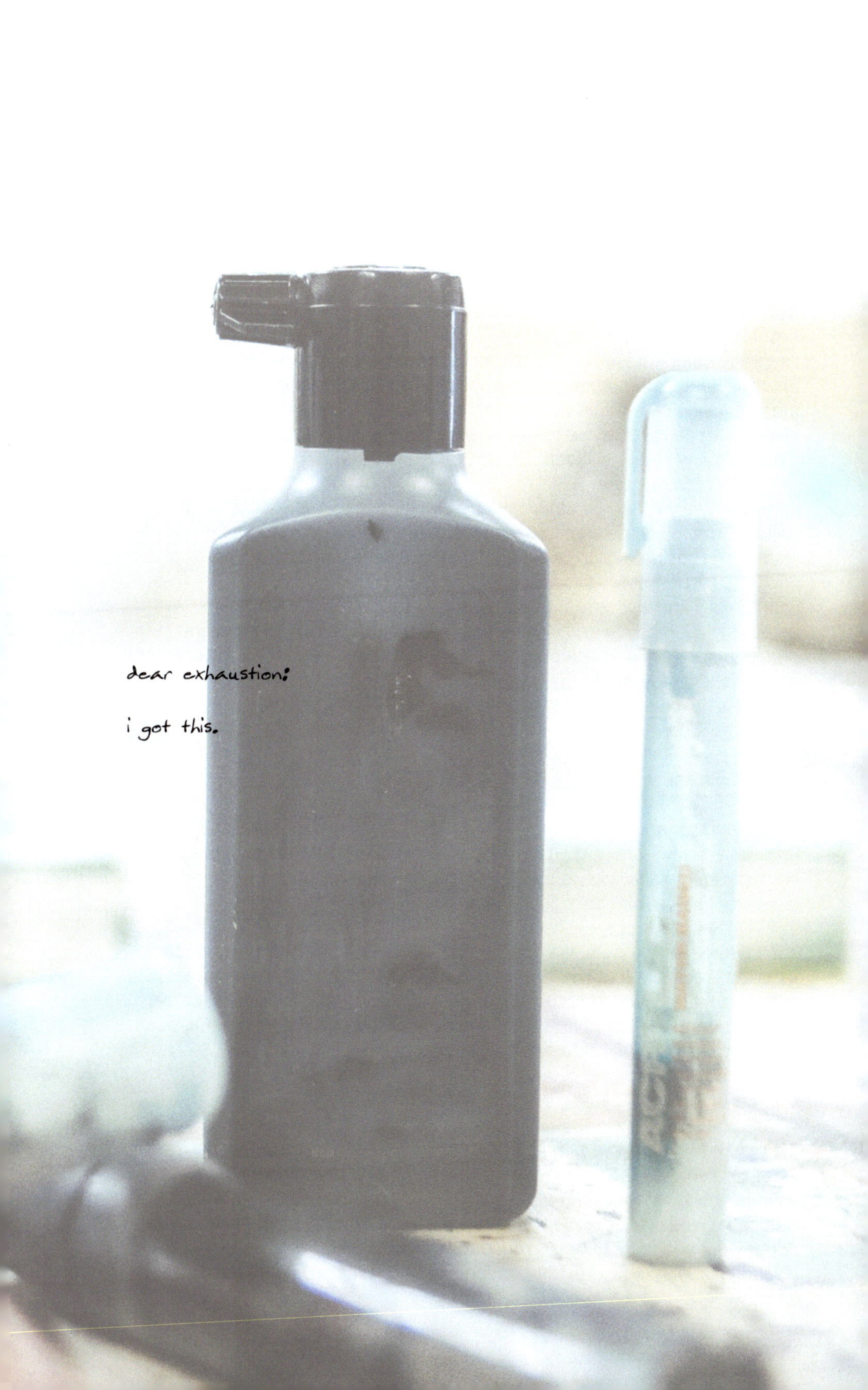

dear exhaustion:

i got this.

be now/

i'm pretty quiet - most of the time. yet i'm capable of volcanic eruptions of energy and frenzied moments of eruption. it's just that i'm better with a brush than i am with verbalizing my words. i have said this repeatedly, but in many ways it can be hard for me to talk about my work. that's why i paint - i'm trying to show you how i feel.

i am constantly asked by other artists how i'm able to make art a full-time gig. generally my answer is not taken well. it is not pretty, + it's not easy. i didn't start with a business plan, a studio, fancy business cards, or an art blog.

i don't really know when i started. but it was slow. i have a family, so i couldn't just jump ship and announce i was an artist. i looked for clients during the day, took phone orders for unfortunate pleated khakis by evening, and, if i could stay awake, would paint a little after that - then do it all over again the next day. Honestly, not the peak of my artistic career, but it was part of the journey.

if i had only known then…

actually - i did, and so do you. you know it now, + you can feel it - so do it. do what you love - now. do it at night. wake up two hours early. make it your second job. replace your television schedule with a making stuff schedule. whatever you have to do. do it. now.

don't figure it out - because you won't. i still haven't; no one has. don't wait for clients. don't wait to be debt-free. don't wait for the right situation, for things to settle down, for your kids to go to school, leave the house, or get out of diapers. don't wait for less hours at work. don't wait for summer. don't wait for winter. don't wait to settle down. don't wait.

every day you wait is a day you won't get back.

the world is full of people and corporations who claim to be authentic, creative, game-changing, innovative, inspiring, and paradigm-shifting. sounds great, but that's not good enough. i want to be with/ work with/ collect the work of someone who shows fall-down, crazy-stupid love for his or her work and want to be surrounded by people who are alluring, beguiling, blazing, bursting, epic, frenzied, ravenous, and volcanic. i want passion to erupt.

be now. be active. it surprises people /

be/

as for what inspires me, sometimes i honestly have no idea. i do know that painting is my way of communication.

in general, i am inspired by those who look the world in the eye and say, "back off, i've got this." those that don't slouch or turn around when the path gets too rough. i'm inspired by those who start in their garage. i'm inspired by the idea of making you fall in love with something unexpected.

what will inspire you? who will you choose to be today?

will the task be too big? will you choose to say "back off, i've got this," or will you choose to actually just back off, because no one cares or will see what you're doing anyway?

chose option one. whether you have an impact on one person or a thousand, your work is worth creating. you were given your talent for a reason. you are where you are for a reason.

the path may look long and weary or even like an unmarked trail.

anyone can walk the paved trail. in fact, we all walk the paved trail and seem to end up in the same place.

i want the overgrown, unmarked trail. the one with ripe berries, scampering creatures, unexpected bursts of wild flowers, twists and turns, and places unknown. i want to emerge up with a cuts, bruises and swollen memories to show for my effort. i want to hear the score ding and stars fly off the screen. i want to find the hidden treasures along the way.

i want to burst out of the trail into the field at sunset and run to my destination. i want to fall down breathless at the end of the journey knowing i didn't miss a thing.

i want to do it all over again.

i want to be surprised. /

**no one
can do
what you do,
exactly the way
you do it.**

alexandra franzen

want to share a story about being something?

send me a note at kent@kentyoungstrom.com.

want to share an image on instagram or twitter?

use #besomethingmakesomething + follow me on @kentyoungstrom

want to see what i make?

visit experience.kentyoungstrom.com

www.ingramcontent.com/pod-product-compliance
Lightning Source LLC
Chambersburg PA
CBHW040513290326
41930CB00036B/115